CHRISTMAS CHEER

ISBN 978-1-4234-9470-6

HAL•LEONARD®
CORPORATION

7777 W. BLUEMOUND RD. P.O. BOX 13819 MILWAUKEE, WI 53213

Visit Hal Leonard Online at
www.halleonard.com

BABY, IT'S COLD OUTSIDE

from the Motion Picture NEPTUNE'S DAUGHTER

By FRANK LOESSER

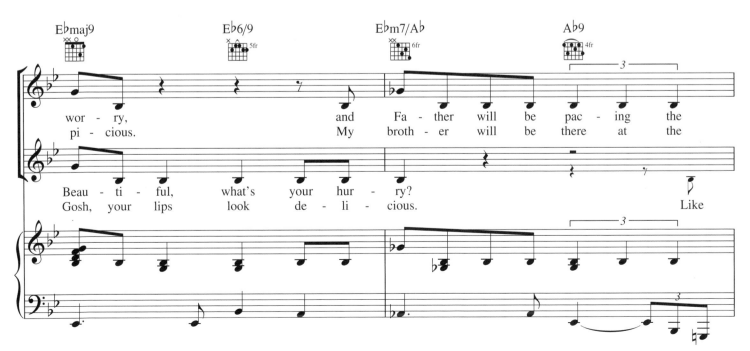

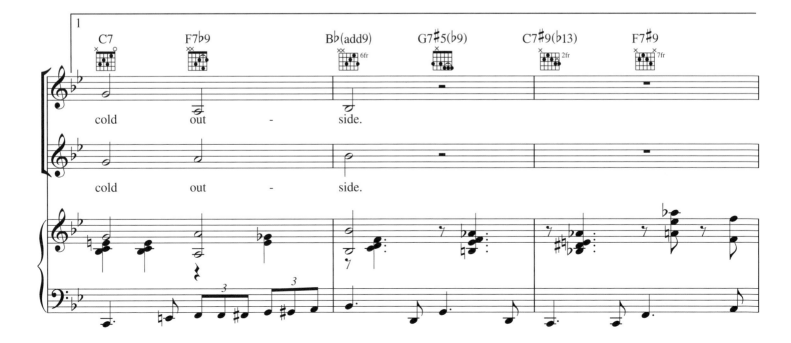

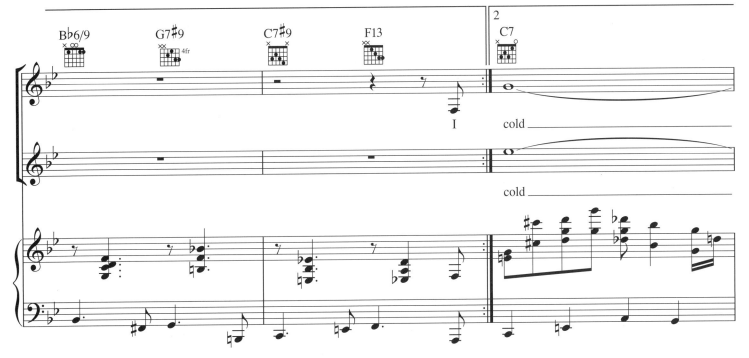

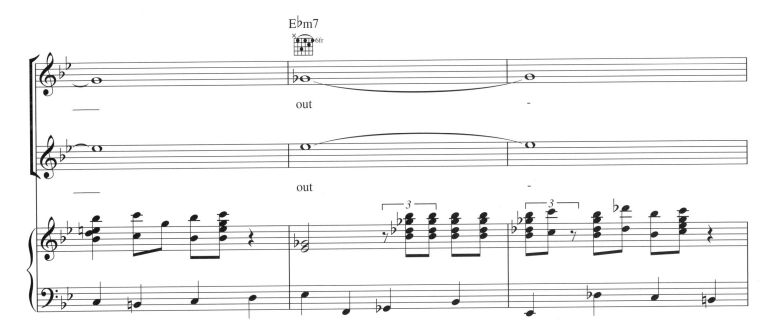

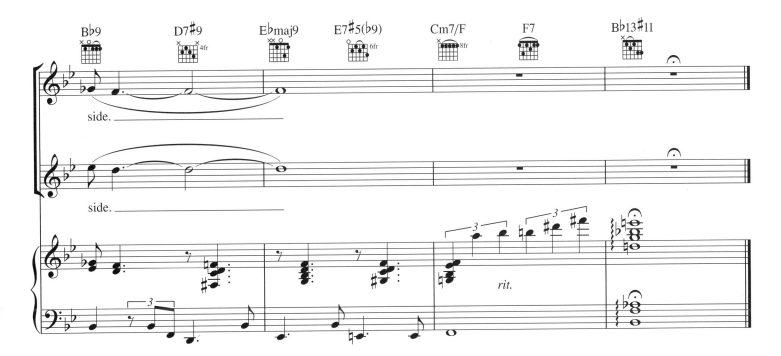

CAROLING, CAROLING

Words by WIHLA HUTSON
Music by ALFRED BURT

With a lilt

Car-ol-ing, car-ol-ing, now we go; Christ-mas bells are ring-ing!
Car-ol-ing, car-ol-ing. through the town; Christ-mas bells are ring-ing!

Car-ol-ing, car-ol-ing, through the snow; Christ-mas bells are ring-ing!
Car-ol-ing, car-ol-ing, up and down; Christ-mas bells are ring-ing!

Joy-ous voic-es sweet and clear, Sing the sad of heart to cheer.
Mark ye well the song we sing, Glad-some tid-ings now we bring.

Ding, dong, ding, dong, Christ-mas bells are ring-ing!

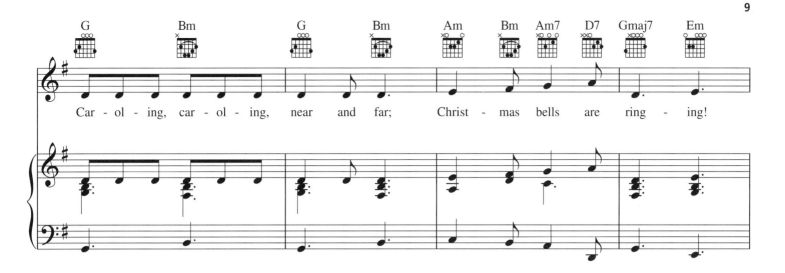

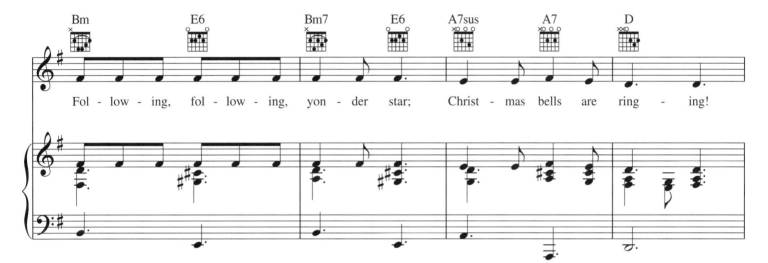

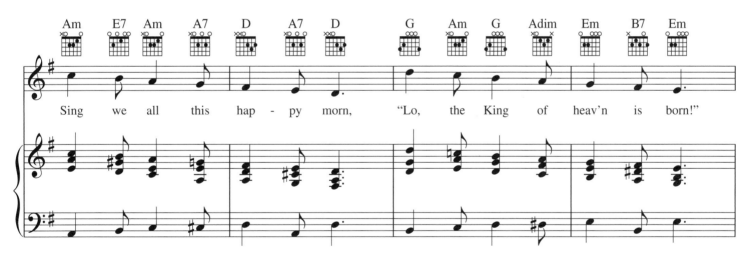

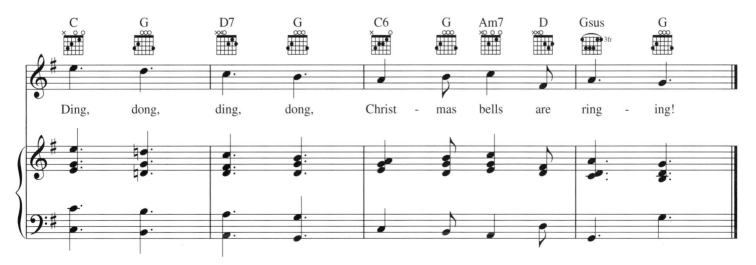

FELIZ NAVIDAD

Music and Lyrics by
JOSÉ FELICIANO

Fe - liz Na - vi - dad. _____ Fe - liz Na - vi -

dad. _____ Fe - liz Na - vi - dad. Prós - pe - ro

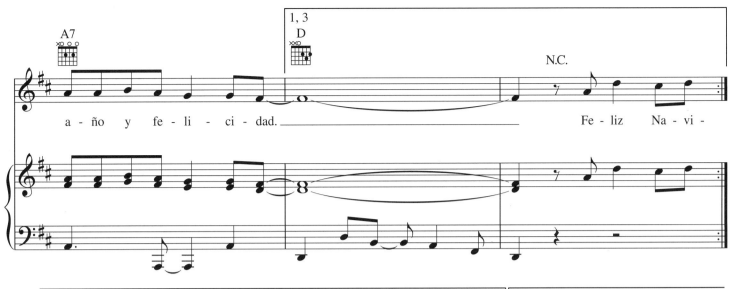

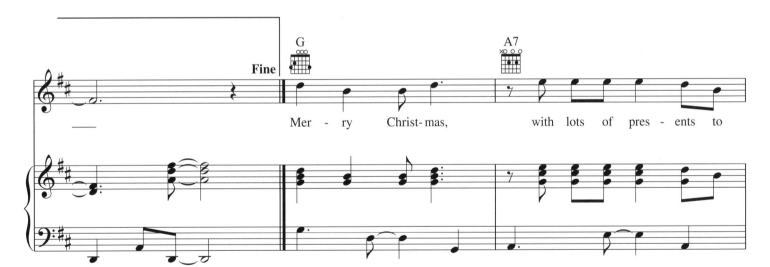

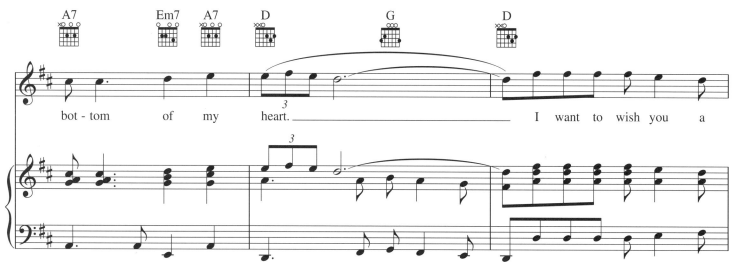

bot - tom of my heart. _____ I want to wish you a

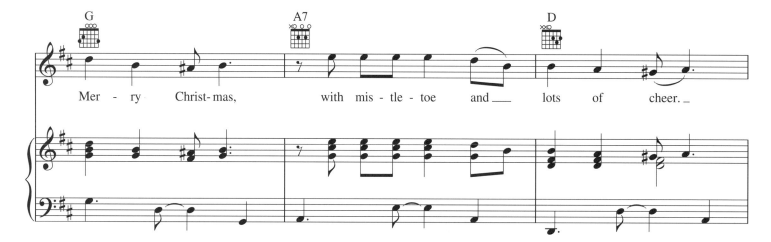

Mer - ry Christ-mas, with mis - tle - toe and ___ lots of cheer. _

With lots of laugh - ter through - out the years from the

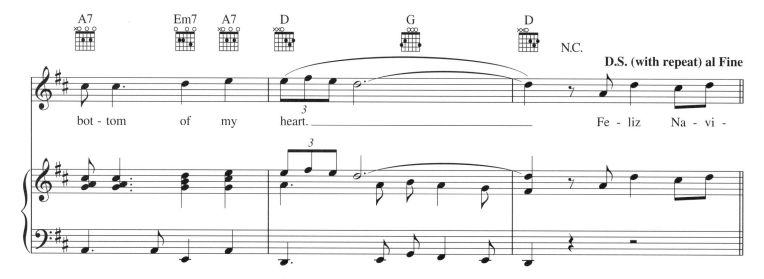

D.S. (with repeat) al Fine

bot - tom of my heart. _____ Fe - liz Na - vi -

HAPPY HOLIDAY

from the Motion Picture Irving Berlin's HOLIDAY INN

Words and Music by
IRVING BERLIN

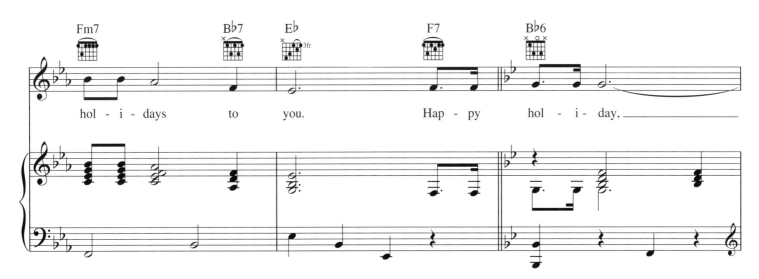

A HOLLY JOLLY CHRISTMAS

Music and Lyrics by
JOHNNY MARKS

Moderately bright

Have a hol-ly jol-ly Christ-mas, it's the best time of the year.

I don't know if there'll be snow, but

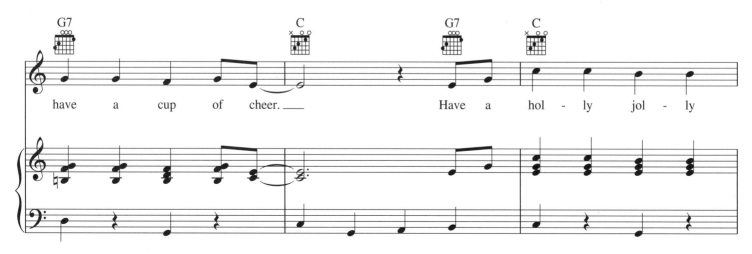

have a cup of cheer. Have a hol-ly jol-ly

Christ - mas, and when you walk down the street, ___

say hel - lo to friends you know and ev - 'ry - one you

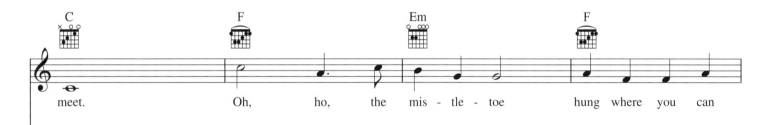

meet. Oh, ho, the mis - tle - toe hung where you can

see. Some - bod - y waits for you, kiss her once for

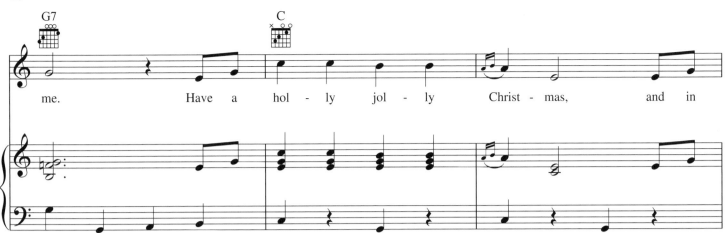

me. Have a hol - ly jol - ly Christ - mas, and in

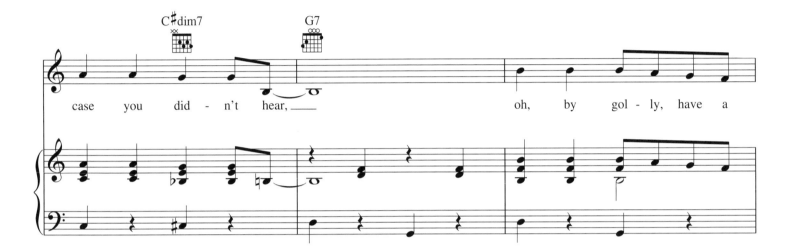

case you did - n't hear, _____ oh, by gol - ly, have a

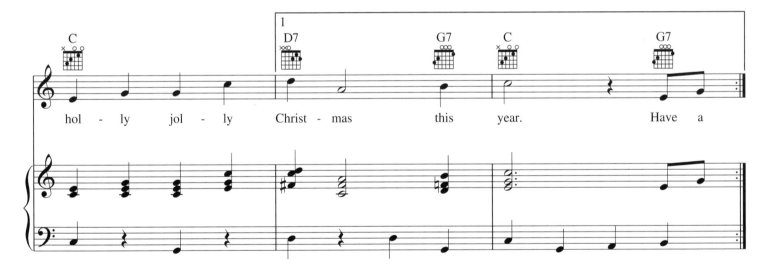

hol - ly jol - ly Christ - mas this year. Have a

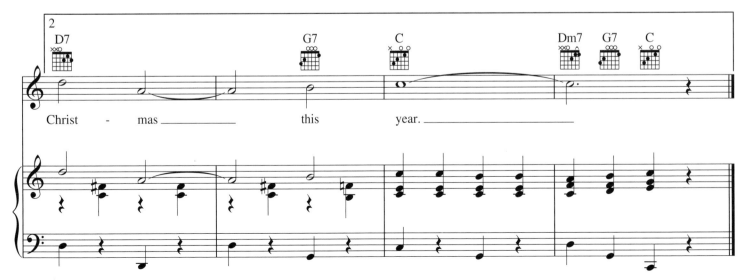

Christ - mas _____ this year. _____

IT'S BEGINNING TO LOOK LIKE CHRISTMAS

By MEREDITH WILLSON

Moderately

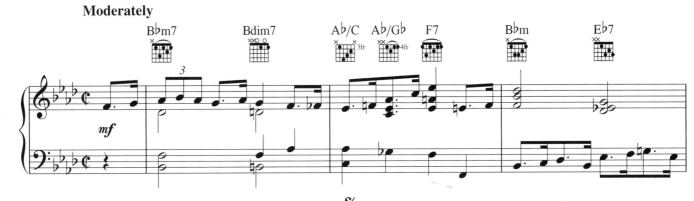

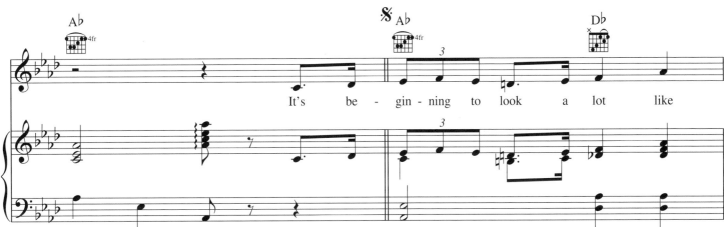

It's be - gin - ning to look a lot like

Christ - mas, ev - 'ry-where you go;

Take a / There's a

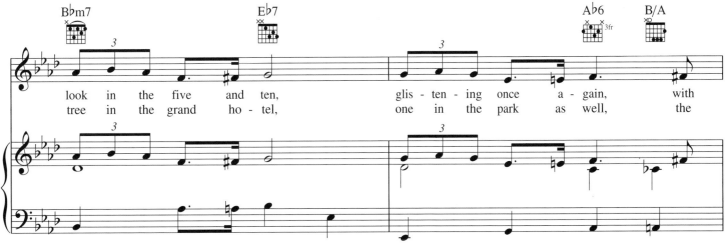

look in the five and ten, glis - ten - ing once a - gain, with / tree in the grand ho - tel, one in the park as well, the

door. A pair of hop-a-long boots and a pis-tol that shoots is the

wish of Bar-ney and Ben. Dolls that will talk and will go for a walk is the

hope of Jan-ice and Jen. And Mom and Dad can hard-ly wait for

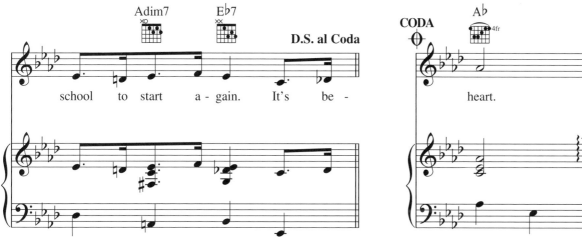

school to start a-gain. It's be-

D.S. al Coda

CODA

heart.

THE MOST WONDERFUL TIME OF THE YEAR

Words and Music by EDDIE POLA
and GEORGE WYLE

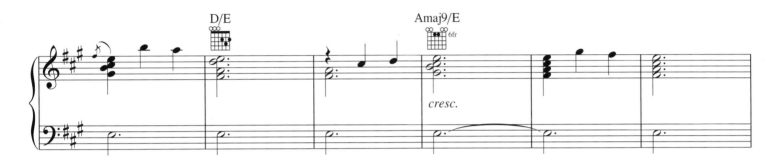

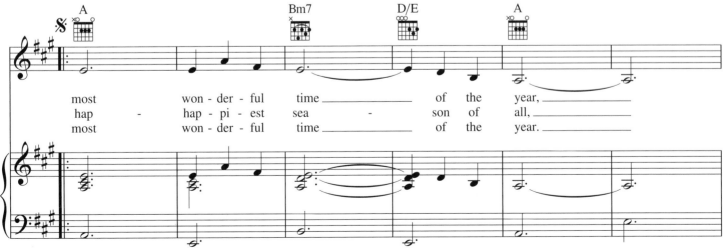

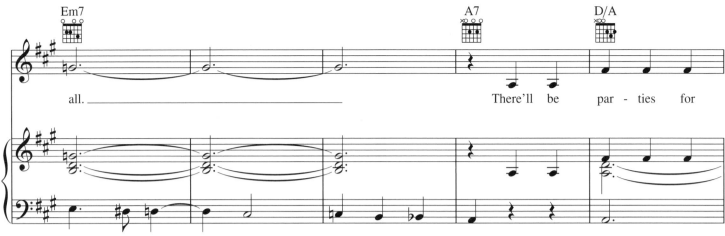

all. _____ There'll be par - ties for

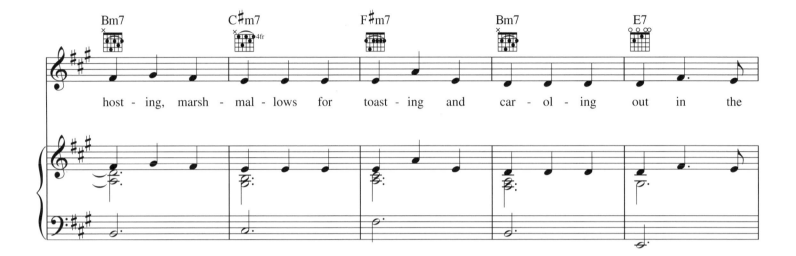

host - ing, marsh - mal - lows for toast - ing and car - ol - ing out in the

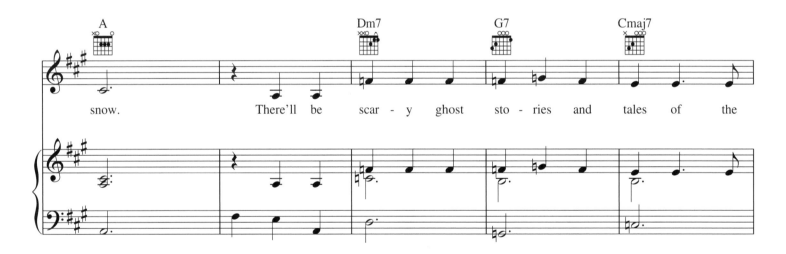

snow. There'll be scar - y ghost sto - ries and tales of the

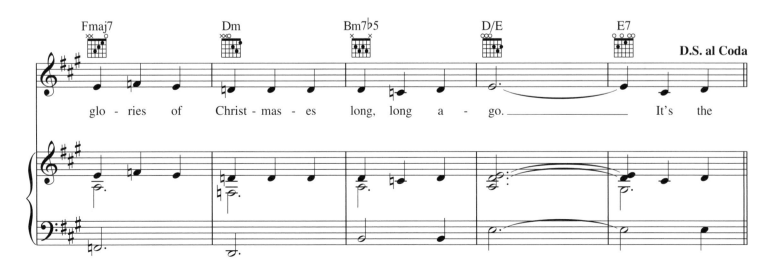

glo - ries of Christ - mas - es long, long a - go. _____ It's the

D.S. al Coda

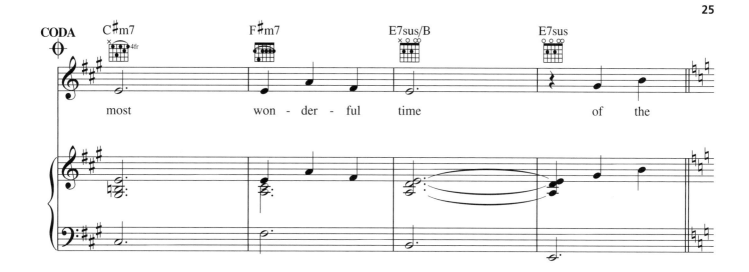

most won - der - ful time of the

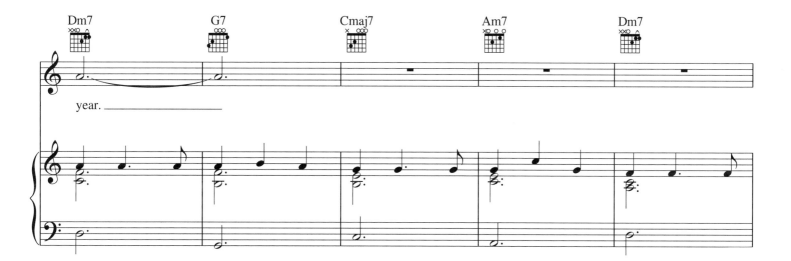

year. _____

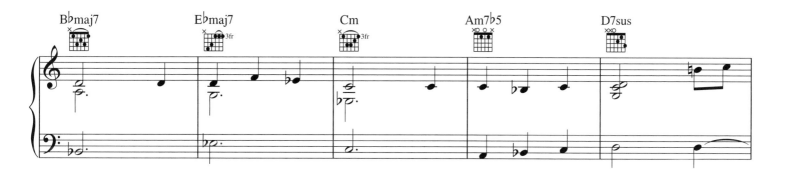

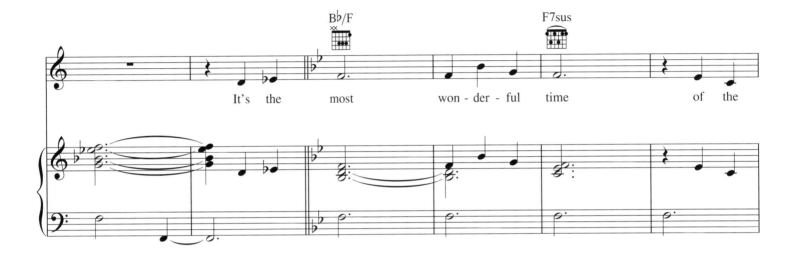

It's the most won - der - ful time of the

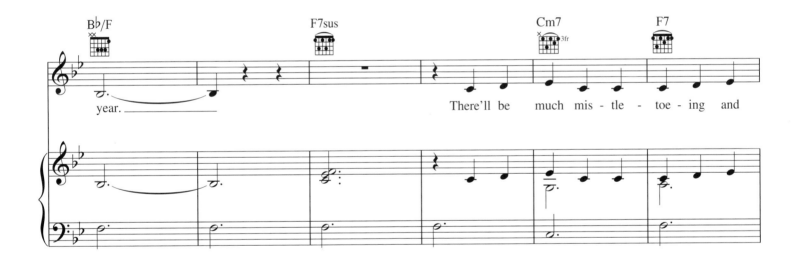

year. There'll be much mis - tle - toe - ing and

hearts will be glow - ing when loved ones are near.

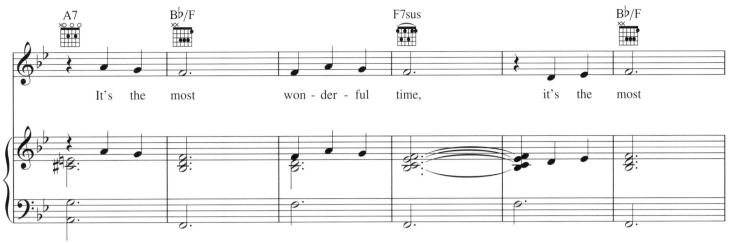

It's the most won-der-ful time, it's the most

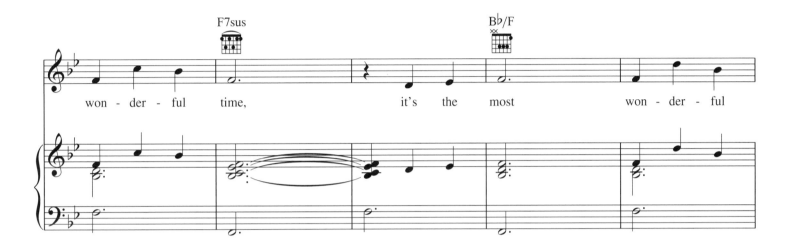

won-der-ful time, it's the most won-der-ful

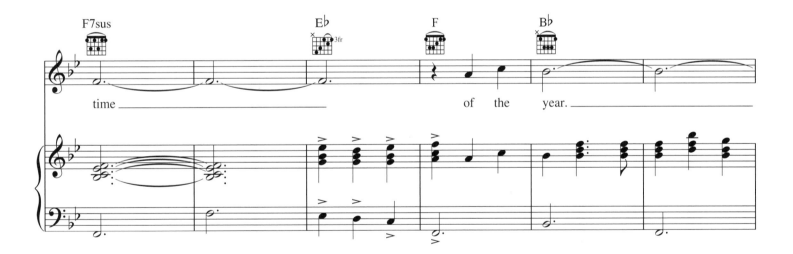

time _____ of the year. _____

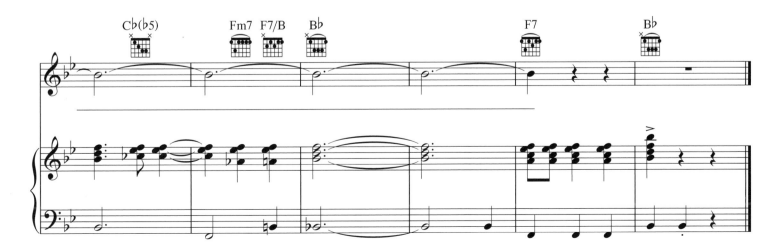

WHITE CHRISTMAS
from the Motion Picture Irving Berlin's HOLIDAY INN

Words and Music by
IRVING BERLIN

The sun is shin - ing, the grass is green, __ the

or - ange and palm trees sway. There's nev - er been such a

day in Bev - er - ly Hills, L. A.

But it's De - cem - ber the twen - ty - fourth, _____

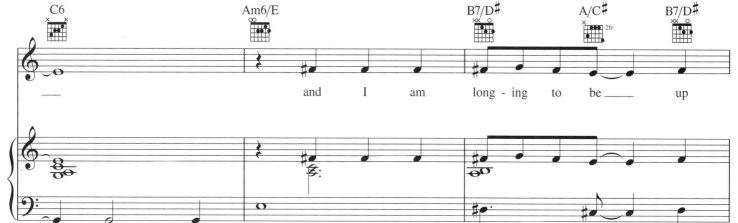

___ and I am long - ing to be ___ up

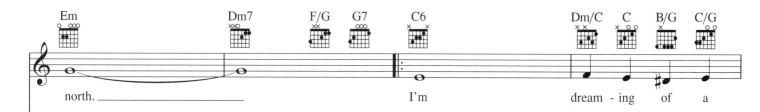

north. _____ I'm dream - ing of a

rit. *a tempo*

white Christ - mas, just like the

ones I used to know, _____ where the

tree - tops glis - ten and chil - dren lis - ten to

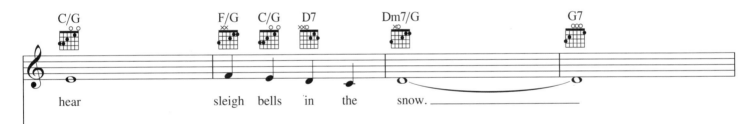

hear sleigh bells in the snow. _____

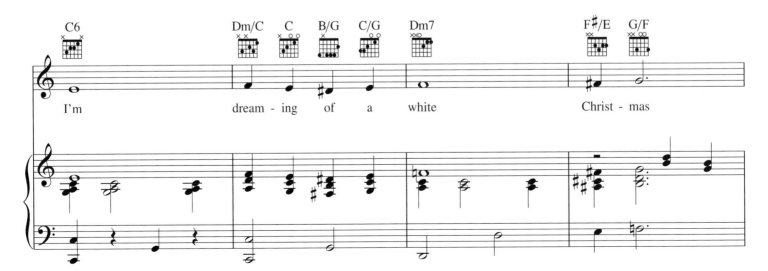

I'm dream - ing of a white Christ - mas

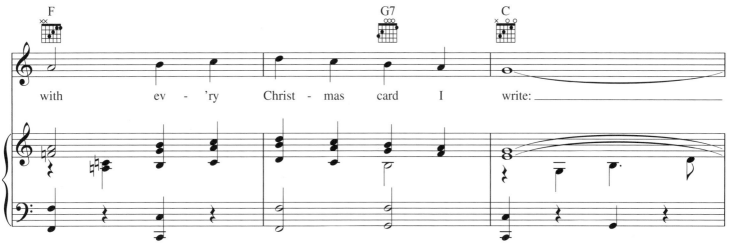

with ev - 'ry Christ - mas card I write: _____

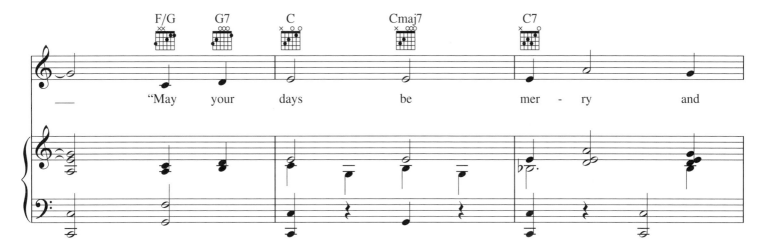

_____ "May your days be mer - ry and

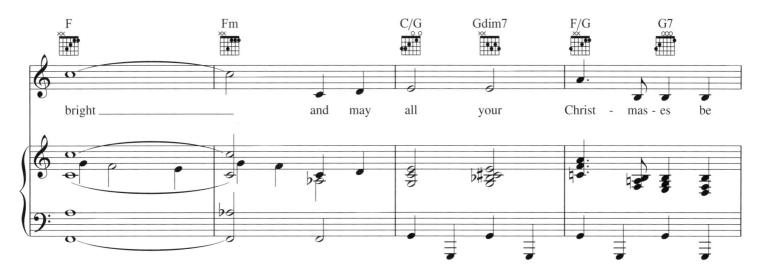

bright _____ and may all your Christ - mas - es be

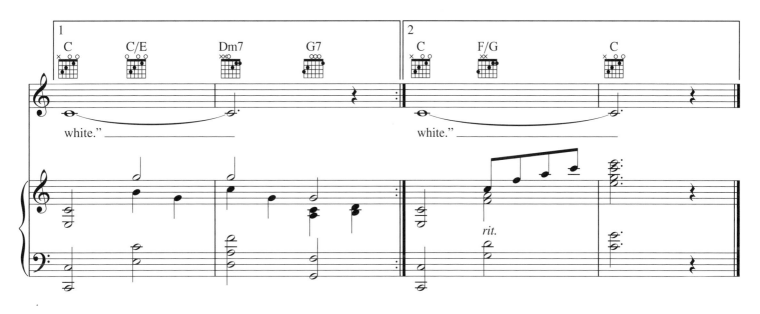

white." _____ white." _____

rit.

THE ULTIMATE SONGBOOKS

HAL•LEONARD

These great songbook/CD packs come with our standard arrangements for piano and voice with guitar chord frames plus a CD.

The CD includes a full performance of each song, as well as a second track without the piano part so you can play "lead" with the band!

PIANO PLAY-ALONG

1. Movie Music
00311072 P/V/G $14.95

2. Jazz Ballads
00311073 P/V/G $14.95

3. Timeless Pop
00311074 P/V/G $14.99

4. Broadway Classics
00311075 P/V/G $14.95

5. Disney
00311076 P/V/G $14.95

6. Country Standards
00311077 P/V/G $14.99

7. Love Songs
00311078 P/V/G $14.95

8. Classical Themes
00311079 Piano Solo $14.95

9. Children's Songs
0311080 P/V/G $14.95

10. Wedding Classics
00311081 Piano Solo $14.95

11. Wedding Favorites
00311097 P/V/G $14.95

12. Christmas Favorites
00311137 P/V/G $15.95

13. Yuletide Favorites
00311138 P/V/G $14.95

14. Pop Ballads
00311145 P/V/G $14.95

15. Favorite Standards
00311146 P/V/G $14.95

16. TV Classics
00311147 P/V/G $14.95

17. Movie Favorites
00311148 P/V/G $14.95

18. Jazz Standards
00311149 P/V/G $14.95

19. Contemporary Hits
00311162 P/V/G $14.95

20. R&B Ballads
00311163 P/V/G $14.95

21. Big Band
00311164 P/V/G $14.95

22. Rock Classics
00311165 P/V/G $14.95

23. Worship Classics
00311166 P/V/G $14.95

24. Les Misérables
00311169 P/V/G $14.95

25. The Sound of Music
00311175 P/V/G $15.99

26. Andrew Lloyd Webber Favorites
00311178 P/V/G $14.95

27. Andrew Lloyd Webber Greats
00311179 P/V/G $14.95

28. Lennon & McCartney
00311180 P/V/G $14.95

29. The Beach Boys
00311181 P/V/G $14.95

30. Elton John
00311182 P/V/G $14.95

31. Carpenters
00311183 P/V/G $14.95

32. Bacharach & David
00311218 P/V/G $14.95

33. Peanuts™
00311227 P/V/G $14.95

34. Charlie Brown Christmas
00311228 P/V/G $15.95

35. Elvis Presley Hits
00311230 P/V/G $14.95

36. Elvis Presley Greats
00311231 P/V/G $14.95

37. Contemporary Christian
00311232 P/V/G $14.95

38. Duke Ellington – Standards
00311233 P/V/G $14.95

39. Duke Ellington – Classics
00311234 P/V/G $14.95

40. Showtunes
00311237 P/V/G $14.95

41. Rodgers & Hammerstein
00311238 P/V/G $14.95

42. Irving Berlin
00311239 P/V/G $14.95

43. Jerome Kern
00311240 P/V/G $14.95

44. Frank Sinatra – Popular Hits
00311277 P/V/G $14.95

45. Frank Sinatra – Most Requested Songs
00311278 P/V/G $14.95

46. Wicked
00311317 P/V/G $15.99

47. Rent
00311319 P/V/G $14.95

48. Christmas Carols
00311332 P/V/G $14.95

49. Holiday Hits
00311333 P/V/G $15.95

50. Disney Classics
00311417 P/V/G $14.95

51. High School Musical
00311421 P/V/G $19.95

52. Andrew Lloyd Webber Classics
00311422 P/V/G $14.95

53. Grease
00311450 P/V/G $14.95

54. Broadway Favorites
00311451 P/V/G $14.95

55. The 1940s
00311453 P/V/G $14.95

56. The 1950s
00311459 P/V/G $14.95

57. The 1960s
00311460 P/V/G $14.99

58. The 1970s
00311461 P/V/G $14.99

59. The 1980s
00311462 P/V/G $14.99

60. The 1990s
00311463 P/V/G $14.99

61. Billy Joel Favorites
00311464 P/V/G $14.99

62. Billy Joel Hits
00311465 P/V/G $14.99

63. High School Musical 2
00311470 P/V/G $19.95

64. God Bless America
00311489 P/V/G $14.95

65. Casting Crowns
00311494 P/V/G $14.95

66. Hannah Montana
00311772 P/V/G $19.95

67. Broadway Gems
00311803 P/V/G $14.99

68. Lennon & McCartney Favorites
00311804 P/V/G $14.99

69. Pirates of the Caribbean
00311807 P/V/G $14.95

70. "Tomorrow," "Put on a Happy Face," And Other Charles Strouse Hits
00311821 P/V/G $14.99

71. Rock Band
00311822 P/V/G $14.99

72. High School Musical 3
00311826 P/V/G $19.99

73. Mamma Mia! – The Movie
00311831 P/V/G $14.99

74. Cole Porter
00311844 P/V/G $14.99

75. Twilight
00311860 P/V/G $16.99

76. Pride & Prejudice
00311862 P/V/G $14.99

77. Elton John Favorites
00311884 P/V/G $14.99

78. Eric Clapton
00311885 P/V/G $14.99

79. Tangos
00311886 P/V/G $14.99

80. Fiddler on the Roof
00311887 P/V/G $14.99

81. Josh Groban
00311901 P/V/G $14.99

82. Lionel Richie
00311902 P/V/G $14.99

83. Phantom of the Opera
00311903 P/V/G $14.99

84. Antonio Carlos Jobim Favorites
00311919 P/V/G $14.99

85. Latin Favorites
00311920 P/V/G $14.99

87. Patsy Cline
00311936 P/V/G $14.99

88. Neil Diamond
00311937 P/V/G $14.99

89. Favorite Hymns
00311940 P/V/G $14.99

90. Irish Favorites
00311969 P/V/G $14.99

91. Broadway Jazz
00311972 P/V/G $14.99

92. Disney Favorites
00311973 P/V/G $14.99

93. The Twilight Saga: New Moon – Soundtrack
00311974 P/V/G $16.99

94. The Twilight Saga: New Moon – Score
00311975 P/V/G $16.99

95. Taylor Swift
00311984 P/V/G $14.99

96. Best of Lennon & McCartney
00311996 P/V/G $14.99

FOR MORE INFORMATION, SEE YOUR LOCAL MUSIC DEALER,
OR WRITE TO:

HAL•LEONARD® CORPORATION

7777 W. BLUEMOUND RD. P.O. BOX 13819 MILWAUKEE, WI 53213

Visit Hal Leonard Online at **www.halleonard.com**

Prices, contents, and availability subject to change without notice.

Disney characters and artwork © Disney Enterprises, Inc.

0810